# *Would You Rather Eww Edition*

Canggu Publishing

© Copyright 2019 - All rights reserved.

The content contained within this book may not be reproduced, duplicated or transmitted without direct written permission from the author or the publisher. Under no circumstances will any blame or legal responsibility be held against the publisher, or author, for any damages, reparation, or monetary loss due to the information contained within this book. Either directly or indirectly. You are responsible for your own choices, actions, and results.

Legal Notice:
This book is copyright protected. This book is only for personal use. You cannot amend, distribute, sell, use, quote or paraphrase any part, or the content within this book,
without the consent of the author or publisher.

Disclaimer Notice:
Please note the information contained within this document is for educational and entertainment purposes only. All effort has been executed to present accurate, up to date, and reliable, complete information. No warranties of any kind are declared or implied. Readers acknowledge that the author is not engaging in the rendering of legal, financial, medical or professional advice.

The content within this book has been derived
from various sources. Please consult a licensed professional before attempting any techniques outlined in this book.

By reading this document, the reader agrees that under no circumstances is the author responsible for any losses, direct or indirect, which are incurred as a result of the use of the information contained within this document, including, but not limited to, — errors, omissions, or inaccuracies.

# How To Play...

1) Have two or more people around (the more the better).

2) The person holding the book asks the question and the person listening HAS to answer one of the two options (no skipping).

3) Take turns asking questions (don't keep the book to yourself).

4) That's it, have fun!

## Would You Rather...

Have nails that smell like blue cheese OR Eat cheese that smell like dirty socks?

---

Floss your teeth with floss that's already been used OR Gargle your mouth with mouthwash that's already been gargled by someone else?

## Would You Rather...

Drink a cup of someone else's sweat OR Eat a bowl of someone else's boogers?

---

Pick up your phone from inside the toilet after dropping it when you've just finished going OR Have your face washed with toilet water when the water is clean?

## Would You Rather...

Have free unlimited used underwear OR Free unlimited used toothbrushes?

---

Give your grandpa a foot rub at the end of the day when he's just taken off his shoes and socks OR Put sunscreen all over your grandma's body in summer?

## Would You Rather...

Wear a stranger's underwear OR Lick your gym teacher's armpit after doing sports?

Be in the Guinness Book of World Records for having the biggest ear wax in your ear OR Having the loudest fart ever recorded?

## Would You Rather...

Pluck an old man's ear hair OR Wax an old lady's leg hair?

---

Jump into a pool full of monkey poop that smells like chocolate OR Whale pee that smells like apple juice?

## Would You Rather...

Drink the toilet water of your neighbour OR The water inside a fish tank?

---

Have a teaspoon of salt in everything you drink OR A teaspoon of pepper in everything you eat?

## Would You Rather...

Wear the underwear you're wearing now for the rest of the week OR The shirt you're wearing now for the rest of the month?

---

Sleep next to a wasp nest for a night OR Swallow five cockroaches?

## Would You Rather...

Play cricket with a baguette as the bat OR Soccer where the ball is a beehive?

---

Use melted chocolate as moisturiser OR Tomato sauce as shampoo?

## *Would You Rather...*

Have rubber bands as hair OR Vines as arms?

---

Wear a necklace made of human bones OR An anklet made from monkey's teeth?

## Would You Rather...

Eat pesto pasta from the floor with your mouth OR Eat a bowl of cat food with a spoon?

---

Eat a spicy, jalapeño sponge cake OR Grass flavored brownie?

## Would You Rather...

All your hair on your body fall out OR All your teeth in your mouth fall out?

⬅———————

Have an extra tongue on your forehead OR Roots growing in your gums between your teeth?

## Would You Rather...

Eat one huge scorpion OR One hundred tiny little scorpions?

---

Have the ability to spit on things and burn them with your acidic saliva OR Breathe so hard you can get a flame come out of your mouth like a baby dragon?

## Would You Rather...

Grow hair on your fingernails OR Have fingernails grow from your head?

---

Build a giant, Scottish castle with cutlery and honey with your friends OR A huge tree house with smelted iron with Barack Obama?

## Would You Rather...

Meet your favorite celebrity smelling like stinky armpits or OR Be on a first date with garlic breath?

---

Eat a whole baguette without any drink to go with it OR Drink a tuna and spinach milkshake?

## Would You Rather...

Have nails that are a foot long and always black OR Hair that touches the ground?

---

Everyone have lobster claws for fingers OR Everyone have fish antennas instead of noses?

## Would You Rather...

Be an earthworm in your next life OR A grasshopper?

---

Drink an unknown pink substance that turns you into cotton candy OR A random mushroom from the ground that sends you to another universe?

## Would You Rather...

Use sweet chilli sauce as a face mask OR Drink a shot of sriracha sauce?

---

A bag of almonds covered in beetroots OR A carrot sandwich dunked in soy sauce?

# Would You Rather...

Eat a cheese croissant made from camel's milk OR Eat pasta sprinkled with cheese made from a hippopotamus?

---

Eat curry sardines, bread, and dark chocolate OR Drink a smoothie with sweet chilli sauce, sour cream, and chocolate milk?

## Would You Rather...

Four bullying big brothers OR Four younger yelling sisters?

---

Cut the lawn with a pair of scissors OR Mop the floor with a toothbrush?

## Would You Rather...

Always have snot running down your nose OR Always have the sensation a sneeze is coming on?

---

The top of your head be made out of glass so you can see your brain work OR Your stomach be made out of glass so you can see all your organs?

## Would You Rather...

Eat a goat brain curry OR Deep fried chicken feet?

———————————

Take a shower in warm, pulpy orange juice OR Have a bath in warm, canned tomato chunks?

## Would You Rather...

Eat an anchovy flavored muffin OR A tuna flavored banana?

---

Be a famous scientist for creating an evil bacteria that wipes out half the planet OR An inventor who creates the vaccine but gets no credit for it?

## Would You Rather...

Do a cannonball into a pool filled with maggots OR Bathe in a bathtub full of petrol?

---

Clean the Eiffel Tower with a toothbrush OR Mop the whole Louvre Museum in Paris?

## Would You Rather...

Be bald and have no hair on your body OR Be so hairy you're mistaken for a gorilla sometimes?

---

Have everyone's leftover lunch from school as your lunch every day for a month OR Wear clothes from the second hand store for the rest of the year?

## Would You Rather...

Have spicy nachos cheese thrown all over you OR Cookies and ice cream?

---

Your toothbrush be able to make comments and always tell you how your teeth and gums are doing OR Your pillow be able to sing so you can fall asleep peacefully?

## Would You Rather...

Sleep in a tree house covered in termites for a night OR Sleep in a cave sharing it with hundreds of screeching, black bats?

---

Cry like when you're cutting onions every time you eat food OR Only taste onions every time you sit down to eat food and not cry?

## Would You Rather...

Put a gym sock in your mouth until you pass out OR Help your grandpa pluck his eyebrows?

---

Wear dirty socks and shoes on your hands for a day OR Your underwear on your feet?

## Would You Rather...

Have a finger shaped like a spork OR A finger shaped like a knife?

Feed a rat to a cobra with your bare hands OR Pat a wild eagle with claws as sharp as nails?

## Would You Rather...

Make a snowman with sand and ear wax OR A gingerbread house with cookie dough and tree sap?

⟵――――――――⟶

Paint a drawing using your tongue as a paint brush OR Create a sculpture using honey as glue and your toes instead of your fingers?

## *Would You Rather...*

Go in the ring and have one round with Mike Tyson OR Wrestle with a baby silverback gorilla?

---

Your grandma lick the palm of her hand then slick your hair back in a busy cafe OR Your grandma give you a sloppy kiss on your cheek, leaving lipstick there that won't come off all day at home?

## Would You Rather...

Eat dog vomit OR Eat a fried tarantula?

---

Have a thousand tiny teeth in your mouth like sharks do to chew your food OR Have a thousand tiny eyes like flies do to see a hundred times better?

## Would You Rather...

Be stuck in the sewers over a night OR Be pooped on by an elephant?

Smell like foul milk OR Slimy seaweed?

## Would You Rather...

Have eight limbs like a spider OR A giant tail like a rat?

---

Have two noses on the side of your head and one ear in the middle OR Your eyes on the side of your head and your ears where your eyes are?

## Would You Rather...

Walk a dog that stops to poop every five minutes OR Clean a bird cage that hasn't been cleaned all year?

---

Always have a piece of broccoli stuck between your teeth OR Find a flea every time you eat a cauliflower?

## Would You Rather...

Sleep in a room with a skunk OR Have a hive of bees follow you around all day?

---

Have ear hair so long it dangled out and looked like earrings OR Eyebrow hairs so long they covered your eyes?

## Would You Rather...

Drink a smoothie with six raw eggs OR Eat one raw onion with the skin on?

---

Eat an Oreo that tastes like canned baked beans OR An Oreo that tastes like rotten eggs?

## Would You Rather...

Have melted cheese looking skin OR Boiled spaghetti as your hair?

---

Wash your dog by licking him with your tongue OR Clean him up after pooping using your bare hands?

## Would You Rather...

Eat a fried booger panini OR A cheese burger with worms instead of onion?

---

Wear shoes with a sole made from chewing gum OR Wear a hat made from branch twigs with itchy insects on them?

## Would You Rather...

Eat a raw piece of kangaroo OR A raw piece of rabbit?

⟶

Wear a diaper to the swimming pool instead of speedos OR Be in the swimming pool when ten other people pee around you at the same time?

## Would You Rather...

Take all the cobwebs off the ceilings from your school OR Clean all the teacher's toilets?

---

Find a treasure chest in a lake but get bitten by piranhas as you try to retrieve it OR Find a hidden treasure in the woods but have to get passed a grizzly bear in order to retrieve it?

## Would You Rather...

Drink the water in a pot hole from the rain OR Eat the dead leaves from the tree on your street?

---

Be on a show where they throw pies at you while you run through a maze OR Be the star while you sit on a dunking booth filled with soy sauce?

## Would You Rather...

Drink milk from a cat OR Drink a smoothie made from crushed up insects?

---

Crawl on your hands and legs from school to home through thick snow OR Go down a burning hot metal slide in the middle of summer ten times?

## Would You Rather...

Smell rotten eggs for the rest of the month OR The worst, dirty laundry you've ever smelt for the rest of the month?

---

Wear stinky feet perfume in your birthday party or find worms in your birthday cake?

# The End

www.ingramcontent.com/pod-product-compliance
Lightning Source LLC
Chambersburg PA
CBHW071758080526
44588CB00013B/2288